MY FIRST SPORTS

Basketball

by Ray McClellan

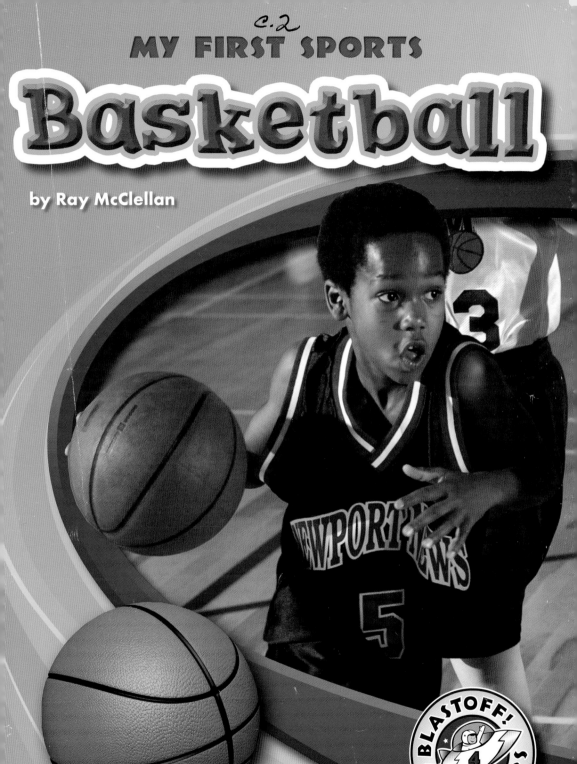

BELLWETHER MEDIA • MINNEAPOLIS, MN

Note to Librarians, Teachers, and Parents:

Blastoff! Readers are carefully developed by literacy experts and combine standards-based content with developmentally appropriate text.

Level 1 provides the most support through repetition of high-frequency words, light text, predictable sentence patterns, and strong visual support.

Level 2 offers early readers a bit more challenge through varied simple sentences, increased text load, and less repetition of high-frequency words.

Level 3 advances early-fluent readers toward fluency through increased text and concept load, less reliance on visuals, longer sentences, and more literary language.

Level 4 builds reading stamina by providing more text per page, increased use of punctuation, greater variation in sentence patterns, and increasingly challenging vocabulary.

Level 5 encourages children to move from "learning to read" to "reading to learn" by providing even more text, varied writing styles, and less familiar topics.

Whichever book is right for your reader, Blastoff! Readers are the perfect books to build confidence and encourage a love of reading that will last a lifetime!

This edition first published in 2010 by Bellwether Media, Inc.

No part of this publication may be reproduced in whole or in part without written permission of the publisher. For information regarding permission, write to Bellwether Media, Inc., Attention: Permissions Department, 5357 Penn Avenue South, Minneapolis, MN 55419.

Library of Congress Cataloging-in-Publication Data
McClellan, Ray.
  Basketball / by Ray McClellan.
     p. cm. – (Blastoff! readers. My first sports)
  Includes bibliographical references and index.
  Summary: "Simple text and full-color photographs introduce beginning readers to the sport of basketball. Developed by literacy experts for students in grades two through five"–Provided by publisher.
  ISBN 978-1-60014-279-6 (hardcover : alk. paper)
  1. Basketball–Juvenile literature. I. Title.

GV885.1.M39 2009
796.323–dc22   2009008186

Printed in the United States of America, North Mankato, MN.   090110   1174

Contents

What Is Basketball?

Basketball is a team sport that began in the United States. It is played by people of all ages. The National Basketball Association (NBA) is the professional league in the United States.

The NBA has helped make basketball popular worldwide. Today, professional leagues exist all around the world.

! fun fact

The Women's National Basketball Association (WNBA) formed in 1996.

Dr. James Naismith, a teacher, invented basketball in 1891. Naismith based basketball on a children's game called **duck on a rock**.

He set up a basket in a gym and let his students shoot a ball at it. Naismith created some basic rules for the game he called "basket ball." The game has changed a lot since Naismith invented it, but it still has the same basic idea behind it.

The Basic Rules of Basketball

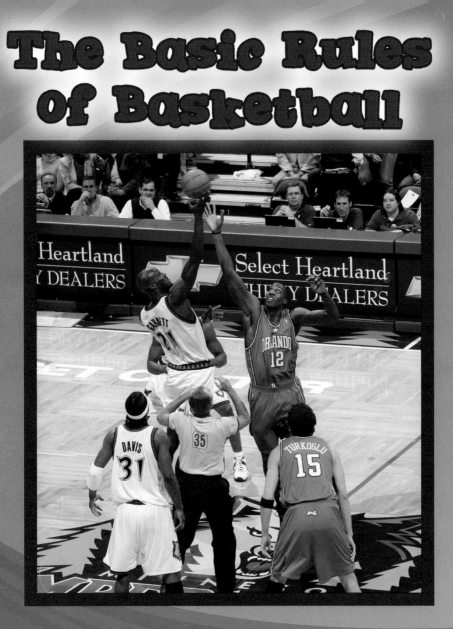

Basketball is a team sport. Five players at a time from each team take the court. They play both **offense** and **defense**. The game starts with a **jump ball**.

An official tosses the ball up at center court. Each team picks a player to jump for it. The team that gets the ball is on offense. The other team is on defense. Defensive players can try to **steal** the ball and **block** shots.

Players on offense get two points for most baskets. They get three points for shots made from behind the **three-point line**. After a **foul**, players may be awarded **free throws**. Each free throw is worth one point.

After a missed shot, either team can go for the **rebound**. The team that collects the loose ball is on offense. After a basket is made, the team on defense gets the ball.

fun fact

A shot clock forces teams to shoot the ball within a set amount of time.

three-point line

Players must **dribble** the ball as they move with it. A player who stops dribbling must pass or shoot the ball. The player cannot start dribbling again. A player who moves without dribbling is called for **traveling** and the other team is awarded the ball.

Fouls take place when a player breaks a rule. Most fouls happen when a defender pushes an offensive player who is shooting the ball.

Basketball Equipment

The ball is the most important piece of basketball equipment. The inner layer of a basketball is rubber. It is filled with air. The outside layer is leather, rubber, or a combination of materials.

A men's basketball measures about 30 inches (76 centimeters) around. A women's basketball measures about 29 inches (74 centimeters) around.

fun fact

Yao Ming is one of the tallest NBA players. He is 7 feet 6 inches (2.3 meters) tall and wears a size 18 shoe.

An NBA basketball court is 94 feet
(29 meters) long and 50 feet (15 meters)
wide. College and high school courts are a
little smaller.

The baskets stand 10 feet (3 meters) high.
There is a **backboard** behind each basket.
Players can use the backboard to bounce
shots into the basket.

Basketball Today

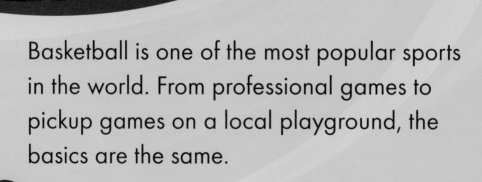

Basketball is one of the most popular sports in the world. From professional games to pickup games on a local playground, the basics are the same.

Players must work as a team to win. They must dribble, jump, pass, and shoot their way to victory.

LeBron James

In the NBA, stars like Kevin Garnett and LeBron James lead the way. Women's league fans cheer for stars such as Candace Parker and Lauren Jackson.

Candace Parker

Stars like these inspire kids and adults around the world to pick up a ball and see what they can do on the court.

Glossary

backboard—the board, made of wood or fiberglass, to which the basket is attached

block—to stop a shot from reaching the basket by hitting it away

defense—the team that does not have the ball and is trying to stop the offense from scoring

dribble—to continuously bounce the ball while moving

duck on a rock—a game in which players place a rock on top of a stump or a stone, then try to knock it off by throwing smaller rocks at it

foul—a rule violation that often results in free throws for the other team

free throw—a shot taken from the free throw line after a foul; defenders cannot try to stop a player during a free throw.

jump ball—the play that begins each half of a basketball game; the official throws the ball into the air and one player from each team tries to tap it to a teammate.

offense—the team that has possession of the ball and is trying to score

rebound—to grab a loose ball after a missed shot

steal—a play in which a defensive player takes the ball from an offensive player

three-point line—a curved line painted on a basketball court that marks the distance where shots are worth three points instead of two

traveling—a call made against a player who moves without dribbling the ball; a traveling call gives the ball to the other team.

To Learn More

AT THE LIBRARY

Brown, Jonatha A. *Basketball*. Milwaukee, Wisc.:
Weekly Reader Early Learning Library, 2004.

Doeden, Matt. *The Greatest Basketball Records*.
Mankato, Minn.: Capstone, 2009.

Gifford, Clive. *Basketball*. New York, N.Y.:
PowerKids Press, 2009.

ON THE WEB

Learning more about basketball
is as easy as 1, 2, 3.

1. Go to www.factsurfer.com.

2. Enter "basketball" into the search box.

3. Click the "Surf" button and you will see a list of
   related Web sites.

With factsurfer.com, finding more information is just a
click away.

Index

The images in this book are reproduced through the courtesy of: GPI Stock / Alamy, front cover, pp. 12, 13, 19; Lisa Blumenfeld, pp. 4-5; Hulton Archive / Getty Images, p. 6; Ty Allison / Getty Images, p. 7; David Sherman, p. 8; Barry Gossage / Getty Images, p. 9; David Dow / Getty Images, pp. 10-11; BLewisphotography, p. 14; John W. McDonough, p. 15; Melissa Majchrzak / Getty Images, p. 16; Matthew Porter, p. 17; Esbin-Anderson / Age Fotostock, p. 18; Garrett Ellwood / Getty Images, p. 20; Andrew D. Bernstein, p. 21.